Greetings from
AROUND
MANCHESTER

A nostalgic trip around the outskirts of Manchester in Picture Postcards.

by
Cliff Hayes

A Memories publication

in association with the

Manchester EveningNews

Published by:
Memories
222 Kings Road,
Firswood,
Manchester M16 OJW
Tel: 0161 862 9399

in association with

© Cliff Hayes

ISBN 1 899181 91 1

Former ISBN 1 872226 39 6

First published 1992 as
Greetings From Around Manchester
This edition published 1999

Printed by: MFP Design & Print
Longford Trading Estate,
Thomas Street,
Stretford,
Manchester,
M32 OJT.
Tel: 0161 864 4540.

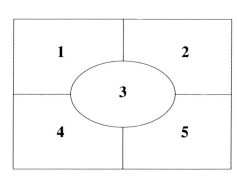

FRONT COVER PICTURES:
1. The Village Flixton about 1900
2. Cross Street, Gorton 1912
3. Higher Openshaw, Ashton Old Road 1935
4. Chester Road Stretford, looking towards Altrincham 1920
5. The Old Cake Shop, Eccles 1906

FOREWORD

The idea of this book came because my collection of postcards and leaflets on Manchester was growing yet I did not have enough on any one area to produce a complete book, as my pal Ted Gray has done with Salford and Eccles. So I thought why not put together a book that touches the areas around the city without dwelling too much on any one place.

Many of us relate to more than one part of Manchester. I live in Stretford, shop in Chorlton, work in Salford, take my daughter to school in Hulme and my wife's family come from the Old Trafford area. So I have connections with five areas of the city, and there are many like me. The really hard part has been working out what is "Around Manchester", how far out to go, where to include and where to leave out.

Altrincham is to me just on the edge of Manchester, yet Altrinchonians spend a great deal of their day telling others that they are part of the 'Cheshire Set' and denying they have ever heard of Manchester. I think the best way is to say that being a Mancunian is a state of mind. If you think you are a Mancunian then YOU ARE A MANCUNIAN.

Manchester only became a city in 1853 and its population was around 100,000. Then Bradford, Rusholme and Harpurhey were added in 1885. Crumpsall, Newton Heath, West Gorton, Openshaw, Blackley, Clayton and the oddly named area Moston-Kirkmanshulme followed 1890. The new century saw Heaton Park, Moss Side, Heaton Norris, Didsbury, Withington and Levenshulme added to the city. A 1901 census counted 540,000 souls to the city of Manchester.

I have included the above areas along with some of the Salford areas and I hope that I have covered most of what people consider is MANCHESTER apart from the city centre. The city centre has been fairly well covered and it will be a change to give the surrounding areas a chance. Anyway there is always another book that could cover the heart of the city.

It is hard for us to imagine how useful the postcard really was. There were few telephones, and the main way of keeping in touch was by postcard. Births, deaths and engagements were all announced by the ubiquitous postcard. "I'm coming round to see you next Tuesday, will you be in?" can often be found on the back of a card.

The areas covered in this book have been placed in alphabetical order, but defining areas is sometimes a little hard. When postcards became very popular the large companies instead of buying photographs from local photographers and producing postcards from them, sent their own photographers into an area, usually just for a day, and he would come back with his notes and it was not unknown for him to make a small mistake. There are one or two in this book where the printed caption is wrong and we have pointed this out. This makes it hard to put some cards in the right areas.

Whitefield is a good example. A card can have Besses o' The Barn on it, yet show a road in Whitefield; and a picture taken only a hundred yards up the road has Stand on the front. These cards have all been grouped under the Whitefield area. So please bare with me if some areas are not strictly correct, or if you think we are a little out.

It has been a very interesting job compiling this book. My wife Sylvia and I have visited EVERY location in the book and stood where the cameraman stood in each case. This has taken us into some remote corners of Manchester but it has been a real eye-opener to see how some areas have survived and just how much others have changed.

So here is a special collection of over 150 old postcards, advertisements, old photographs and anecdotes that I hope will provoke nostalgia and bring back personal memories, or just start a few readers into their own quest to find out more about where they live and work.

I hope you enjoy the book and that the memories brought back are pleasant ones.

Cliff Hayes

If you are interested in finding out more about the history of your area there is no better place to start than your own local library. Eccles, Stretford, Salford, Failsworth etc., all have good Local History Groups and you can find out details about joining from your local library.

I must thank Ted Gray for his help and loan of the postcards and Jim Stanhope for additional postcards. Most cards come from my own collection and I thank the postcard collectors fayre which is held at the Rudyard Hotel on the A6 near Stockport, every last Tuesday in the month, which has helped me enlarge my collection. A final thanks to Mike Shah (my colleague) for his continuous assistance and toleration.

ABOUT THE AUTHOR

Born 1945 and brought up in The Ball O'Ditton, Widnes, when it was proper and part of Lancashire. Educated at Chestnut Lodge Infants, Simms Cross Junior and then Wade Deacon Grammar School in Widnes I then spent 4 years going to night school at the college of Art in Liverpool to study printing, Design and English.

From the age of 13 I was involved in printing, working part-time at a small local printers, then getting an apprenticeship at Swale Press (Widnes Weekly News, Runcorn, Liverpool etc.) then started helping and writing for Mersey Beat and also writing a disc and pop column for the Weekly News.

Letchworth; Tinlings, Prescott: Ship's printer, Canadian Pacific to Canada and Cruising, Shaw Saville on the world trips and Japanese/Australian cruising etc; Book production in Blackpool; newspaper works manager in the Isle of Man; lino operator on National Newspapers (The Daily Mirror, The Sporting Chronicle, The Daily Telegraph etc); computer training and 12 months as print salesman all added to a broad view of every aspect of printing and of life in general. Now settled to writing and local history, Cliff gives talks to groups on local history and can be heard popping up on local BBC radio quite often.

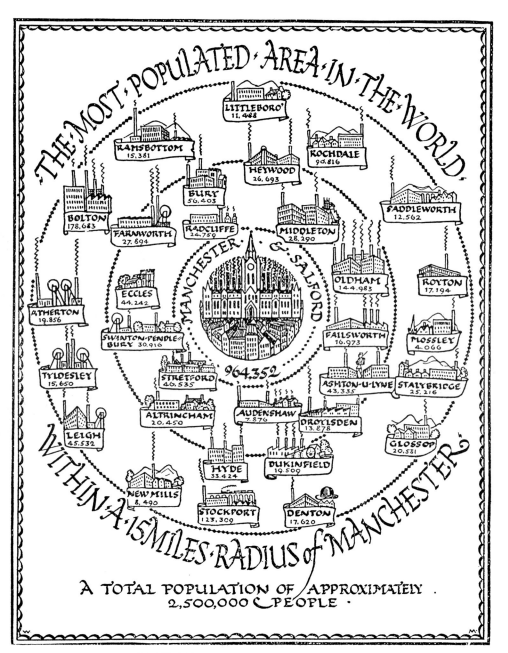

ADVERTISING IN MANCHESTER 1926

ALTRINCHAM

Manchester Road, Altrincham showing the George and Dragon. Still a notorious bend here, but note the width of the road going away to Broadheath. This Lilywhite card from early this century catches the milkman with his three wheeler bike and pristine uniform delivering milk to a very rural Altrincham.

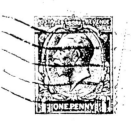

ALTRINCHAM

Altrincham Market in 1915, maybe the War accounted for the sparseness of goods on the stalls. This market was roofed over in 1930 and was only one day a week (Tuesday) until after the Second World War.

Stamford New Road showing the post office, and in the distance the recently completed clock tower. Note the single tram line giving more room in this gas-lit street.

ALTRINCHAM

Stamford New Road in Altrincham in the 1920's, at the junction of the Downs. To the left of the picture is the Downs Hotel. Things did not alter much in those days, and the number 48 tram became the number 48 bus. The sharp-eyed will note that the tram lines just come to an abrupt halt, which of course meant that the trams used to start their journey back on the same line.

Ardwick's proud Empire Theatre on a card in the Grenville series. The Manchester Hippodrome closed down in 1935 and in 1937 this theatre changed its name to The Hippodrome, and continued till about 1960. The open topped tram wending its way past helps date this card as around 1900.

Ardwick Green photographed in 1934 showing the Hippodrome (Empire) with Ardwick's other theatre, the Apollo, which started life as the ABC Cinema, behind the number 34A tram trundling into town.

MANCHESTER HIPPODROME

ARDWICK GREEN

Managing Director	PRINCE LITTLER
Manager	FRED C. BROOKS
Assistant Manager and Press Director	D. BUCKLAND-SMITH

6-0 TWICE NIGHTLY Monday, March 8th, 1943 **8-0**

POPULAR PRICES - INCLUDING TAX

Stalls **3/6 2/6** Circle **3/6 2/6**

Unreserved 2/- Balcony **1/-**

Sats. and Hols., Front Stalls 4/- (Unreserved)

BOOK IN ADVANCE—Box Office Open from 10 a.m.   Phone ARDwick 4101-2

ASHTON ON MERSEY

Ashton Lane in 1904 shows a very picturesque and rural Ashton on Mersey. I wonder what the gentleman with the whiskers, waistcoat and fob watch is waiting for?

View of specially-designed Monkey Mountain in New Centenary gardens, Belle Vue.

BELLE VUE

What a crowd waiting to get into the excitement of Bell Vue.
The uniforms in the queues help date this picture as 1944
and the end of the Second World War in sight. Note the trolly
bus, they were kept in service until the end of the War.

V.   R.

BELLE VUE GARDENS: Mr. Jennison,
proprietor.—In consequence of the unfavourable state
of the weather, and at the request of many persons,
M. JULLIEN, with his UNRIVALLED BAND, have been
engaged to give ONE MORE (the last) MUSICAL FETE !
THIS DAY (Saturday), August 3rd, 1850.—Also, by the kind
permission of Colonel Arthur and the Officers, the splendid
BAND of the Third Dragoon Guards, conducted by Mr. Run-
geling, will perform in conjunction with M. Jullien's great
Orchestra.
  The programme will be composed of Ancient and Modern
Music, with the most popular selections of the last concert,
including "The Derby Galop" and "The Nepaulese Qua-
drille" (which were received with such immense applause),
and n   interesting novelties

BELLE VUE

Belle Vue was started in 1836 by John Jennison as a pleasure grounds with a few animals to see. Then the idea of Firework displays and more animals followed about 1875 and the funfair was added at the end of the last century.

The Palm Court Lounge Hotel at Belle Vue, taken in the 1950's. The large dance hall built at the rear was always full. Note the 'Bobs' and the 'Scenic Railway'. It is difficult for youngsters today to take in how large and how busy Belle Vue was and how much went on there. The cinemas that have replaced it, though good are not any where near as much fun. A VERY MUCH MISSED AMENITY.

BELLE VUE

ZOO & GARDENS, Manchester.
● **BRITAIN'S GREATEST ENTERTAINMENT & SPORT CENTRE** ●

CONSTANTLY extended Wonder Zoo - Glorious Gardens - Brass Band Contests
Speedway Racing - Dancing - Firework Spectacles - Boxing - Wrestling - Boating.
EXHIBITIONS—Largest Hall in North for Trade and Public Exhibitions.
CONGRESSES, MEETINGS, Etc.— Vast King's Hall, seating 7,000.
SPORTS & RALLIES—Mammoth Stadium accommodating 40,000.
DANCES—Coronation Ballroom and other
halls for all social events.

SPECIAL RATES for Organised
Parties of 20 and over, and
experienced assistance in or-
ganising big events. Apply:
Dept. **B.D.** BELLE VUE
(Manchester) LIMITED,
Manchester, 12.
Phone: EASt 1331. Grams:
Bellevue, Manchester.

SOMETHING NEW FOR YOU TO DO, OR SEE ALL DAY - WET OR FINE

Sailors enjoying their leave at Belle Vue. What a mecca Belle Vue was for the people from all over the North of England. I can remember being taken there as a lad, all the way from Widnes, where I lived.

BLACKLEY

Market Street Blackley in the 1950's. Can you make out the advertisement on the wall saying "Drinka Pinta Milka Day" in the days before too much milk was bad for you.

Blackley Village at the end of Market Street, showing its Wilson's Pub with their "Bass" advert, and the shoe repair shop across the square.

BROOK'S BAR

Two views of the Whalley Hotel at Brook's Bar. The Hotel was named because Mr. Brook, who owned much of the land around here, came from Whalley.

This picture of Brooks Bar from 1903 features the horse drawn open top omnibus heading from the Prince of Wales to Chorlton.

Twenty years on and Brooks Bar has not changed much save the trams lines which now dominate the road. Note the controllers cabin in the middle of this busy junction where the Inspector controlled the right of way for his trams.

CHEADLE

The White Hart Hotel in Cheadle with the village church behind it. This Hotel on the famous A34 to London was always a well known Coaching House at the junction of Gatley Road and High Street.

CHEETHAM HILL

Referred to on this card as Cheetham Hill Village, this shot shows the view looking towards Manchester about 1905. The hotel on the right is the Paragon advertising 'Walkers and Humphries' Ales.

CHORLTONVILLE

The Green at Chorltonville showing the Horse and Jockey but much smaller than today. Note the fence and garden around what was the living quarters and now is part of the Pub.

Beech Road, Chorltonville: Very little has changed since this 1910 postcard, the centre of Chorlton had already moved away from here to today's centre. A delivery wagon waits outside the hardware shop, now Beech Road book shop and run by my mate Brian Barlow, well worth a visit. (That plug will cost you a pint, Brian).

CHORLTON-CUM-HARDY

Still recognisable today a 1930's shot of the junction of Barlow Moor Road and Wilmslow Road with the Royal Oak Hotel next to what is now a Nat West Bank. Wade and Wood the butchers were prominent on this corner for many years.

Taken from the car park of the Lloyd Hotel, on Wilbraham Road looking across at John Manners outfitters this 1957 postcard of Chorlton shows a busy suburban shopping street. I wonder how many young lads were dragged like the one in the picture to John Manners for his next school uniform.

CHORLTON-CUM-HARDY

A little further away from the centre of Chorlton this 1930 shot shows Wilbraham Road with the Lloyd Hotel on the right advertising 'Platts' Ales.

POST CARD

THE ADDRESS TO BE WRITTEN ON THIS SIDE

From that same junction looking towards the then busy Chorlton Railway Station. The buildings themselves have not changed much from this late 1920's postcard.

CHORLTON

The Tram depot and terminus on Barlow Moor Road looks busy and bustling on this 1930's postcard. Still referred to as Chorlton Offices.

CLAYTON BRIDGE

This very old photo of the Bay Horse Inn, in Clayton Bridge in 1890. Vauxhall Farm on the left of the picture looking very dilapidated. Clayton Bridge was part of the area known as Medlock Vale.

CLIFTON

A nice composition shot of Clifton from 1913 sent by a Jack Weston staying at Elm House on holiday!

COLLYHURST

The small court yards and the infamous back to back housing in Collyhurst taken before 1900. The camera catches a piece of social history of how people in the poorer areas of the city lived in those times.

DAISY NOOK

Again back to the Clayton Bridge area and a turn of the century picture of Daisy Nook – and the River Medlock. This was a favourite picnic spot for people from all over north Manchester. The Owdabs Cottage Tea Rooms was a very popular place to visit, though it's long gone now and just a lay-by in the road to denote where it was.

Another View of Daisy Nook (1906?) I wonder what the people on the green are doing? The building on the green is referred to as the Bandstand in one leaflet. The white building in the left foreground was Red Bill's Pub and it's still there though it has been a private house since 1935. The area on the right is now Daisy Nook Garden Centre.

DAVYHULME

Lostock Road, Davyhulme just before the First World War. The road and cobbles sweep away to what is now the M62 motorway. The door way at the very right of the picture belongs to the Nags Head Pub.

DIDSBURY

The tram terminus Palatine Road in West Didsbury. It took quite a while to place this picture of the tram on the corner of Lapwing Lane, (just by Inmans Bookshop, in Didsbury) the remains of the station sign can still be seen. I visited this spot recently and they were very busy ripping up the platform and demolishing what was left of the station.

This picture of the Village, Didsbury, looking from the station. Taken before the First World War with the local bobby on his beat having a chat with a shop-keeper.

DIDSBURY

A proud display of blinds on this sunny day in 1908 showing a rural view of Wilmslow Road, Didsbury.

The Old Cock Hotel, Didsbury. The Antique Shop, in this 1930's postcard is now a restaurant.

ECCLES

Barton Road Swing Bridge, Manchester Ship Canal. 11
Weight of Steel 640 Tons. Span 90 Ft.

The 640 ton road bridge at Barton swings open its 90 foot span to let pass an in-coming ship guided by one of the Ship Canal's Paddle Tugs.

Church Street Eccles in 1930. Only just recognisable now it is pedestrianised. The cross in the centre of the picture is till there today, partly hidden by shrubbery.

FAILSWORTH

The Bulls Head on Oldham Road, Failsworth, in the early 1920's. I like the motor bike and side car outside the pub.

Failsworth showing its famous 200 foot cross. St. John's Church looks on a busy Oldham Road.

FALLOWFIELD

An Edwardian Fallowfield with a variety of shops lining the road looking south towards the railway station (now Yates's Wine Lodge). See the brand new car with its N 79 number plate parked outside the 'Grocers & Tea Blenders' I wonder what that car driver would make of our roads now? Apart from 'Shanks's Pony' there are four methods of transport shown in this picture, and that does not include the trains which ran frequently to all the thriving suburbs of Manchester at that time.

FLIXTON

THE INSTITUTE, FLIXTON.
W. H. LONGWORTH, ARCHE

Flixton Institute.

The Flixton Institute was built as a Young Mans' Club specially for the young men of the town. In total it cost £1,250 to build and on 25th February 1909 opened with a Three Day Bazaar to raise the sum of £900 so that the Institute could open free from any debt. In 1914 it closed 'for the duration' and was converted into Wibbersley Hospital No. 2. This postcard is from that period and was issued by the British Red Cross to raise funds for the Hospital. It re-opened again after the war as before. In 1948 when the Local Education Committee took over the running of the club, girls were invited to join for the first time. Today it is known as 'Flixton Youth Club' and is still as popular as ever with the teenagers in the area.

FLIXTON

The photographer has lined up the village children to add charm to this 1900 view of Flixton Village. This was the old centre of Flixton and the building sticking out on the left at the back was the vicarage and is still there and well preserved. Some details worth studying, the little boy sat with his hoop under the Rowntrees & Brooke Bond Tea adverts, the bassinets (prams) and the children's clothes and the boy in cloggs at the front of the group.

THE VILLAGE, FLIXTON

Another postcard of the Village in about 1900. The shop with the writing on the side is now a private house called 'The Village'. The houses next to it went in the widening of Church Road. The Greyhound Hotel on the right is still there, although rebuilt, and the whole scene is still recognisable today.

FLIXTON

What a rural scene, The Red Lion in Woodsend Road on the right and Bannisters shop and the newsagents on the left. Three young trees shade a lone gent waiting for the omnibus around 1910.

Woodsend Road again just before World War Two. The newsagents has gone to a private house and general store. The three trees now have a railing around them and a telephone box has replaced the bus shelter. J.A. Smith from the Post Office in Flixton published this card. Going to this spot today you will find it completely changed. The Red Lion has been rebuilt further back, and the three trees still are still standing, but everything else in this picture has gone.

FLIXTON

Flixton House — how the Council intended it all to turn out

OFFICIAL OPENING OF FLIXTON HOUSE AND GROUNDS, FLIXTON

28 September, 1935

2.30 P.M.

Formal Opening of house and grounds and unveiling of Memorial Tablets.

3.15 P.M.

Sports for the pupils of County maintained schools in the district.

7.30 P.M.

Fireworks Display.

Music will be rendered by the Cadishead Public Band until 7.30 p.m.

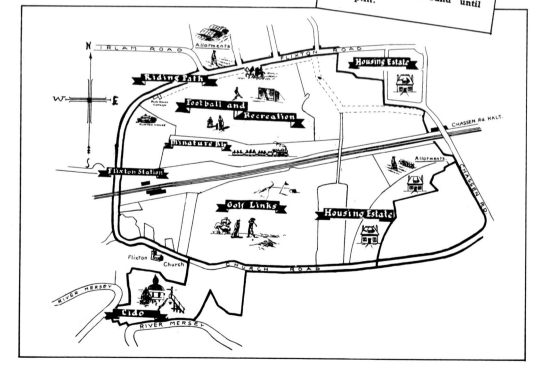

GORTON

Two pictures of a Street 'Victory Party 1945' in Gorton. First it was the children's party then the grown-ups. Can you spot the radio on the chair in both pictures. I wonder if anyone recognises any of the happy grins. "That's me under the cross" states the proud writer of this card. These people have just come through a hard war, and now they are enjoying their 'Victory' celebration, it is a pity there are not get-togethers like this these days. I can remember The Queen's Jubilee in 1970, and we had a street party in Firswood, we had a great day.

The End of Gorton Works taken from *The Guardian*

West Gorton and the imposing Monastery towers over the rest of Gorton Lane. The toy shop and the other shops on the right hand side of the picture have now gone, replaced by houses, and they are thinking of turning the Monastery into luxury apartments

GORTON

The spire of St. James' Church on Hyde Road watches over Sunny Brow Park, Gorton, and the youngsters there. This postcard dated about 1900 records the childrens dress as well as this popular park. I can not see today's children wearing the flat caps and heavy clothing shown here. That really is something that has changed for the better.

Hyde Road viewed from the corner of Cross Street. This is one picture that can still be recognised today as these buildings are still standing and still used. On the right is Gorton Evangelical Church.

HARPURHEY

The terminus of the horse-drawn tram route to Harpurhey was outside the "Farmyard Hotel", Barnes Green on Rochdale Road. The trams started running in 1881 and electric trams took over in 1901. I think this is one of the last or possibly the last horse-drawn tram, pictured here ready for the journey back to the city. The tram-car is of the Edes Patent Reversible type.

HEATON PARK

THE OSTRICH   HEATON PARK

Bury Old Road and the Ostrich Pub
with its fine views across Heaton
Park. The Ostrich is still there but the
building with the spire has gone.
Heaton Park was one of the largest
areas to be taken under the city's
wing as a public park. It was purchased
in 1902 for an amazing cost of £23,000
for the 640 acres park and Hall. One
of the last Earls of Wilton whose
family had occupied the Hall since it
was built in the 18th century was
rather eccentric and insisted that when
any of his staff had any spare time,
they were made to work on his
unbelievable 4 mile brick wall which
surrounded the whole estate.

The house in Heaton Park

Walker's Warrington
and Falstaff **ALES**

A good shot of the Yorkshire House Hotel, which stood on the corner of Medlock Street and River Street in Hulme, in the early 1920's. Walker's Warrington Ales and Burton Ales and Stout are well remembered names but those who think Larger is a modern import look at the top corner of the Hotel and see the Walker's British Larger Beer advert.

HULME

Sometimes the camera means to record an imposing building or wide street and ends up being cherished for the small details and advertisements it captures by chance. This is one of those. It is a postcard showing the corner of City Road and Gt. Jackson Street, Hulme. E. Webb's Tobacconists shop provides lots of memories, and advertising slogans - Players' Digger Tobacco, Marcel Cigars, 'Pick a Piccadilly', and who would believe the slogan "For Your Throats Sake, smoke Craven A" these days. Reece & Sons, advertising themselves as 'Men of Letters' is across the road, they were of course Signwriters. Next door to them 'A Chambers and then the Butchers, all frozen in time as World War II is just starting.

Hulme 1925

HULME

Stretford Road, Manchester

Stretford Road, Hulme and almost in Town. The white building with the dome was Pauldens before it burnt down and moved into the City Centre. Can you see the Singer Sewing Machine shop on the left

Studying the advertisements dates this card to the week. It is Chorlton Road and Stretford Road in Hulme at the end of April 1939. There is a poster stating that Gypsy Petulengro will appear at Pauldens the next week and an advert for Rail Excursions to see the Chester Cup (always the first week in May).

46

LEVENSHULME

Cringle Brook, Levenshulme

Very early this century 1902 or 1903 and the open space that was known as Cringle Fields was later bought by the City of Manchester in 1913 to create a public park to be laid out formally for the enjoyment of the general public. The 1914 War held everything up and in the end this corner, where Cringle Brook flowed through the Park was left wild. This card was used as a Christmas card in 1904 by Mr & Mrs H. Howard of The Hurst, Grange Avenue, Levenshulme.

POST CARD

For INLAND Postage this Space, as well as the Back, may now be used for Communication.
For FOREIGN Postage the Back only. (Post Office Regulation.)

The address only to be written here.

With hearty
Christmas Greetings
and every good wish for the
New Year,
from
Mr. & Mrs. H. R. Howard.

The Hurst,
Grange Avenue,
Levenshulme.   Xmas, 1904

Miss F. Estill,

Wellfield House,

Barton-on-Irwell.

LEVENSHULME

This is 14 Crompton Road, Levenshulme, in March 1930. We know that because Eve, who lived there, tells of a photographer knocking and offering, for half a crown (2/6d), twelve postcards of her newly completed house. We went to see if the house was still there and it looks almost the same, although the pavement has been finished now.

Albert Road Levenshulme, about 1910, shows an up-market and very well kept Albert Road, with mature trees.

48

Best known now as the road leading to Asda (or Dales as it is now called). This Edwardian card shows Kirkmanshulme Lane as a quiet cobbled road.

GAS

WILL DO THE

HEAVY WORK

YOU CAN DO THE

" REST "

LONGSIGHT

Still recognisable is the Slade Lane junction on Stockport Road, with the London railway line going over the A6 in the background. Reading the adverts there was boxing at the Free Trade Hall with Kid Lees topping the bill. This picture taken in the early 1920's.

It is good to be able to compare this shot with the last one. Almost the same view just 200 yards nearer to Manchester and about 15 years later. Stockport Road about 1935.

MOSS SIDE

An Edwardian postcard showing a sedate and genteel Alexander Park, Moss Side. The tennis courts, greenhouse, and formal gardens drew many visitors to this lovely tree lined park, where people could enjoy a bit of fresh air, in what was becoming a very industrialised Manchester. And how the kids loved the duck pond.

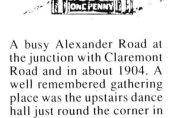

A busy Alexander Road at the junction with Claremont Road and in about 1904. A well remembered gathering place was the upstairs dance hall just round the corner in Claremont Road.

MOSS SIDE

The tram depot on Princess Road, Moss Side, at the turn of the century, and three staff to each tram. These three stand proudly next to their well turned out tram before setting off for Clayton and Old Trafford via Piccadilly. The young lad on the right was officially a trainee, but spent most of his time running to change the points or turning the heavy pole pantograph.

NEWTON HEATH

Oldham Road in Newton Heath and Parr's Bank on the corner of Dean Lane.

NEWTON HEATH

Daisy Bank, Newton Heath and a quite modern card about 30 years ago, the two neat young ladies smiling for the camera helped date this picture as the early 1960's.

This picture taken from Oldham Road, Newton Heath, looking down Church Street towards All Saints Church. Now called Old Church Street, this was one of the main shopping areas of Newton Heath.

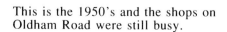

This is the 1950's and the shops on Oldham Road were still busy.

NORTHENDEN

Palatine Road in Northenden in the
1950's. Love the petrol sign on the
right hand side.

OLD TRAFFORD

A very nice early picture of Trafford Bar before the start of this century. Talbot Road on the left led to the Lancashire Cricket ground and Chester Road on the right led to White City, then referred to as the Botanical Gardens.

The White City at Old Trafford was not just a Grey Hound track. As this 1900 post card shows it was a real Pleasure Gardens with lots of attractions for your 6d entrance fee. "Next performance 5.15 p.m." says the board on the right. The entrance portals have survived and stand all spruced up at the new White City Retail Park on Chester Road, that is on this spot now.

OLD TRAFFORD

The junction of Talbot Road and Seymour Grove, Old Trafford, viewed from down Talbot Road. The white fronted building on the left is the Trafford Cinema. It closed down in the 1960's and then it spent many years as a car auction room. At the moment it is empty and derelict. Postcard from the late 1930's.

Seymour Grove leading from Trafford Bar to Chorlton. Pictured here around the late 1930's. The large house on the left is now the site of the Toll Gate Public House.

One last look at Trafford Bar this time from down Seymour Grove. Pictured here in about 1890. The block of shops is still there.

OLD TRAFFORD

HULLARD PARK, OLD TRAFFORD

Well known and popular park was Hullard Park, Old Trafford pictured here in about 1903. Like many other parks, Hullard Park once had a lovely bandstand which it lost in the 1960's.

To celebrate the end of the war Manchester Corporation decorated one tram and this illuminated tram (called the Victory Tram) was a cheerful sight all over the network. Here it is pictured heading up Chester Road towards Manchester from Trafford Bar.

OPENSHAW

OPENSHAW – was one of the heaviest industrial areas in Manchester with vast factories including The English Steel Corporation, Crossley Engines, several Breweries and this factory selling Pearl Barley, Lemonade, and the famous Atora Suet.

This junction of Ashton Old Road, Openshaw, is hardly recognisable today. Only the William Deacon's Bank building on Pottery Lane corner and the white building on Grey Mare Lane corner are still standing. The Britannia Hotel on the other corner and the shops on the left have all gone. A. Longworth's Wines & Spirits; and Singletons Tripe shop were in this block. You can just see a little of the Hand & Heart pub. When they were pulling this block down in the early 70's this public house made its name in local folk history by giving free drinks 'until the pub ran dry!'

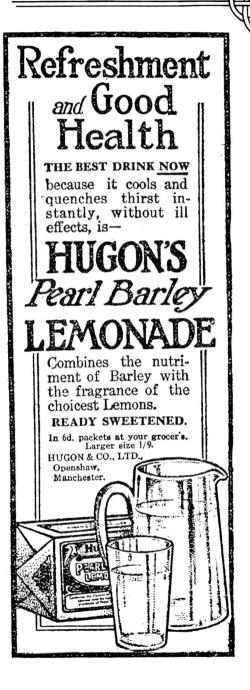

Refreshment and Good Health

THE BEST DRINK **NOW** because it cools and quenches thirst instantly, without ill effects, is—

HUGON'S *Pearl Barley* LEMONADE

Combines the nutriment of Barley with the fragrance of the choicest Lemons.

READY SWEETENED.

In 6d. packets at your grocer's. Larger size 1/9.
HUGON & CO., LTD., Openshaw, Manchester.

OPENSHAW

Further up Ashton Old Road and into Higher Openshaw. The Half Way House Hotel stands guard over the junction of Fairfield Road on the right and Ogden Lane on the left. The Hotel is now closed and boarded up. Another 200 yards further along on the right is the Co-op Building, still standing, but minus its two fancy minarets.

PATRICROFT

Liverpool Road Patricroft and the tram from Whitefield trundles back to town. I like how the shop spills out on to the pavement with all the bits and bobs hanging up outside. It looks like one of those shops that sold everything! This picture is from about 1905.

PEEL GREEN

GREETINGS FROM

LIVERPOOL ROAD

THE LIBRARY

PEEL GREEN

LIVERPOOL ROAD

PEEL GREEN ROAD

POST CARD

This is a post war postcard with four fine views of a neat Peel Green. Two views of Liverpool Road taken from the same spot look both ways. Top left looking towards the Unicorn Hotel plus the Old Library (top right) and Peel Green Road.

PLATT FIELDS

Platt Lane on the corner of Yew Tree Road, Platt Fields, showing what was built as the 'Wilbraham Estate'. See the small 'STOP' sign for the trams hanging over the road. A Seymour Mead's shop on the corner. Seymour Mead was a well known name all over Manchester, founded in 1865 by T. Seymour Meade it made its reputation by never bulking out (or adulterating) its tea or coffee like some of the more unscrupulous dealers did.

PRESTWICH

Prestwich Village and a fine shot from around the late 1890's. I expect this was a posed shot as the cyclist and passers-by are all looking towards the camera. Just in passing can you make out the advertisement for Casket Cigarettes "Delightful To Inhale" 3d per packet. Casket, what an apt name Prestwich for cigarettes.

PRESTWICH VILLAGE.

PRESTWICH

Prestwich and Bury New Road about 1900, taken at the corner of Chapel Street (late George Street). The church across the road has now gone. I wonder what the Scotsman is doing fully kilted on the corner. By the way Browzers Bookshop is one road up and round the corner, pop in and tell him we sent you.

Valuable Leasehold Property in Prestwich.

By Messrs. CAPES and SMITH, on Friday the 9th day of August, 1850, at half-past six o'clock in the evening, at the Red Lion Inn, Prestwich, subject to such conditions as will be then produced:

ALL those TWO newly finished and substantially-erected MESSUAGES or DWELLING-HOUSES, with the garden, ground, and other conveniences thereunto belonging, situate in Butterstile-lane, in Prestwich, about three miles from Manchester, and near the new turnpike road leading from Manchester to Bury. The site of the said messuages, including the garden ground, contains in the whole 2,200 square yards of land or thereabouts. The premises are held for the residue of a term of 999 years, commencing from and created by an indenture of demise dated the 23rd day of June, 1849, and are subject to a yearly rent of £22 18s. 4d. thereby reserved, and to the performance of the covenants and agreements therein contained.

Further information may be obtained from the auctioneers, or from Messrs. WHITLOW, RADFORD, and WHITLOW, Solicitors, No. 2, St. James's Square, Manchester.

Bury New Road again, this time showing Sedgely Park, captioned 'The Village Sedgely Park' taken shortly after the Second World War and looking towards Whitefield.

RUSHOLME

Just after the First World War and Wilmslow Road, Rusholme, is dominated by the clock tower of the Congregational Church now gone.

This view now no longer exists as these shops were knocked down for the motorway. Plenty of people remember Altrincham Road, Sharston as a pleasant shopping area.

A newly-constructed roundabout on Princess Road, Sharston

SALFORD

Cross Lane Salford was reputed to have more pubs per yard than anywhere else in the north. This one "The Prince of Wales Feathers" was at the end of Cross Lane and the landlady Mary Willoughby was a local character. Pictured here in 1920 with her regulars.

A fine shot of Eccles New Road, Salford in the early 1920s. A wonder why they were all walking the same way? Perhaps to Church.

SALFORD

The captions states "The Drill Hall Cross Lane", but this building was better known as Cross Lane Barracks. Taken about 1902 looking towards Pendleton. I wonder why the Union Jack is flying at full mast?

Another card of the Cross Lane Barracks and the board outside says its the home of the 3rd Volunteer Battalion of the Lancashire Fusiliers. The Home Guard used the barracks during the second world war.

3ᴿᴰ BATTALION LANCASHIRE FUSILIERS DRILL HALL, SALFORD.   Copyright.

MR. FOX, Victoria Bridge Inn, Salford, begs leave to intimate to his Friends and the Public that he has ENGAGED, in addition to other talent, Mrs. FOXCROFT, Mr. MORRA, and Mr. SIMPSON, Pianist.— Director of the music, Mr. Morra.

STRETFORD

A fine postcard of the Old Cock Hotel on the very edge of Stretford taken about 1900. This was also as far as the Manchester Carriage Company ran their horse drawn omnibuses and their depot, last used in 1877, was inside the arch on the right. This is the only surviving depot of the Manchester Carriage Company, and the Hotel and archway are still to be seen today, although Hardy's Ales are long forgotten.

This card from about 1898 shows Stretford Public Hall, on Chester Road, privately built by John Ryland twenty years earlier; it contained the first Lending Library in the area. In 1886 a public baths was added to the complex. In 1911 the Hall was purchased by the Council from the Exors of the late John Ryland, it was grandly titled Stretford Public Hall with Assembly Room and Organ. The Talbot Hotel has now gone, and the Civic Theatre is closed to the public

STRETFORD

LONGFORD COFFEE HOUSE, CHESTER RD. STRETFORD

This building looks like a public house, but it was the Longford Coffee House on Chester Road, Stretford, built by John Ryland to encourage temperance in the area, and especially in his workers. This part of Stretford remained more or less unchanged from the end of the last century to the middle of the sixties when the Arndale Centre was built. Where the Longford Coffee House was is more or less MacDonald's now.

This picture is taken from almost the same spot as the last one, but 50 years later. When you travel down Chester Road, Stretford today, and pass the Arndale Centre on the seven lane wide dual carriageway, it is very hard to imagine that this was Chester Road in the early 1960's. The scooter and van pass down a busy road thronged with bustling shops ALL GONE! only the two towers, the Civic Hall and St. Ann's R.C. Church remain of this picture. St. Ann's Church was built in November 1863 but was not consecrated till four years later. The site was given by Humphrey de Trafford and he also picked up the £24,000 bill for building it.

STRETFORD

A leafy traffic-free Edge Lane, in Stretford looking towards Chorlton. Taken about 1910 although it is hard to date and could be earlier. The wall on the left belongs to Longford Park, the Hall there has been let fall into a sorry state. There are moves at the moment to try to save Longford Hall, I do hope they succeed. I remember going to some Antique Fairs and other functions and it was a lovely hall.

Edge Lane, Stretford.

A view of people enjoying Longford Park, Stretford. The Park and Hall were formerly the residence of John Ryland and was purchased in 1911 after a Poll of the ratepayers, who "to their credit be it said, by a large majority took the golden opportunity of preserving this natural woodland park for all time". The picture was taken around the time the park was first opened. I can't stress how much Longford Hall means to the residents of the area. I remember standing alongside the drive in 1977 and watching the Queen drive past to attend the Silver Jubilee Garden Party given in her honour in the gardens.

STRETFORD

Longford Park and the fountains in the gardens taken about 1913. During the First World War Longford Hall was turned into a Recuperation Hospital and this card was sent by a soldier from that hospital. Note the shorthand and the fact that the censor got hold of the card and has decided that something was not in the interests of the country.

If you stand where this photograph was taken you would be looking into the entrance of the Arndale Centre in Stretford, with Argos, and Buckinghams Bingo on your left, and the Post Office on your right. It had recently opened as a post office across the road from J. Raw. Chemist & Optician when this picture was taken about 1930, you can just see the Post Office sign sticking out on the right of this picture.

STRETFORD

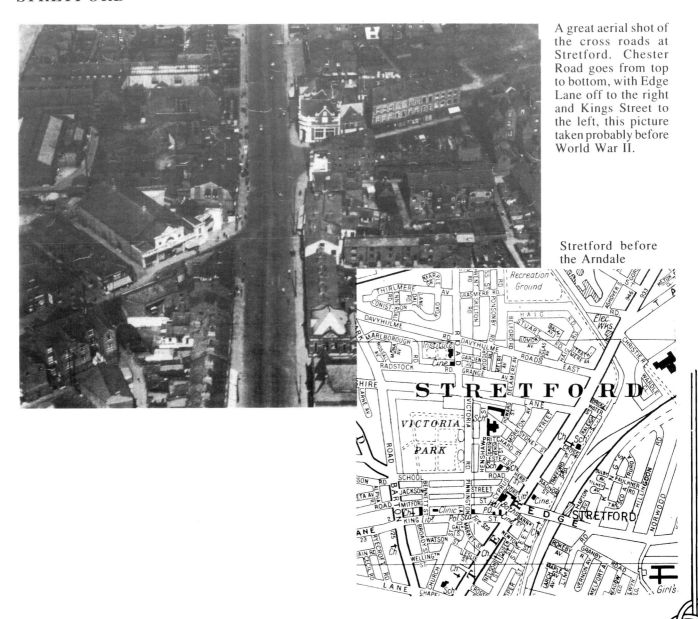

A great aerial shot of the cross roads at Stretford. Chester Road goes from top to bottom, with Edge Lane off to the right and Kings Street to the left, this picture taken probably before World War II.

Stretford before the Arndale

STRETFORD

The Borough of Stretford Charter Celebration September Sixteenth 1933

COUNCIL OFFICES ERECTED IN 1887

THE NEW TOWN HALL, STRETFORD

NEW TOWN HALL—BACK VIEW

STRETFORD

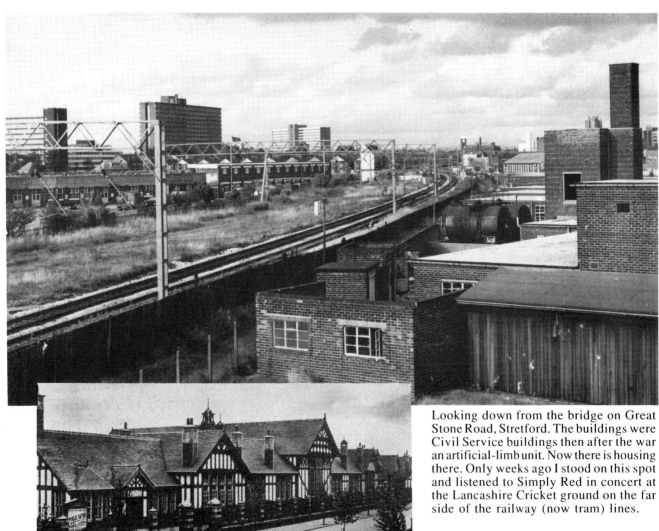

ELEMENTARY SCHOOL, SEYMOUR PARK, OLD TRAFFORD

Looking down from the bridge on Great Stone Road, Stretford. The buildings were Civil Service buildings then after the war an artificial-limb unit. Now there is housing there. Only weeks ago I stood on this spot and listened to Simply Red in concert at the Lancashire Cricket ground on the far side of the railway (now tram) lines.

URMSTON

What an imposing building was Urmston Baths with its splendid glass dome, and elegant lamps on either side of the main entrance. The pool inside was more circular than oblong.

Inside Urmston Baths, with local people enjoying the amenities.

URMSTON

A nice composite card from the late 1940's showing the beauty of Urmston. A little postcard licence includes Barton, Davyhulme and Eccles on this card.

The corner of Station Road and Gloucester Road, Urmston, taken some time in the 1940's. 'Johnsons' the Cleaners and Goulds Shop on the left.

A card from J. W. Ride showing Flixton Road Urmston 1909. The local Co-op shop is on the left, and is still there but replaced with a new building, the other smaller shops are still the same.

Another locally published card from J. W. Ride whose shop was on Flixton Road, Urmston. It shows Station Road at its junction with Church Road to the left and Stretford Road to the right. This picture taken in about 1908.

VICTORIA PARK

St. John Chrysostom's Church in Victoria Park, looking down Anson Road. The Foot Hospital is now on the left of the picture where the trees are.

Victoria Park was originally a private estate built in the 1840's for the cotton and shipping magnets who wanted to live out of the city. The church itself was not built until 1877 and the first vicar was Rev. William Marsden. In 1904 the church was destroyed by fire and restored by John Ely the Architect who attended this church (he also designed Whitworth Park and St.Mary's Hospital). Amongst the many famous people who have lived in Victoria Park, are Sir Charles Halle, the Pankhursts, Ford Maddox Brown, Richard Cobden M.P. and many others. Up to 1926 there were toll gates at the entrances to the area and elderly gate keepers on duty to check who came in and out.

Besses O' Th' Barn, Whitefield

The Junction Hotel at the junction of the Bury and Radclifte Roads looking towards Bury. Behind is the junction of Bury New Road and Bury Old Road. This was always a busy road you can see the policeman ready on point duty. It is even busier now being just a quarter of a mile north of junction 17 on the M62.

Going towards Bury and you find Church Lane, Stand. A pleasant card of the lane in about 1920 and the good citizens of that area probably on their way to All Saints Church at the top of the lane.

THE MAYFAIR CINEMA

SOUVENIR
JANUARY 1936

TUESDAY and WEDNESDAY,
January 7th and 8th

"BULLDOG JACK"
"SHOW KIDS"

AND STRONG SUPPORTING PROGRAMME.

Thursday, Friday and Saturday,
January 9th, 10th & 11th

ENORMOUS ATTRACTION

Dick Powell, Ruby Keeler and Pat O'Brien in

"FLIRTATION WALK"

WHITEFIELD

Stand Church, Whitefield.

Joseph Jackson, Printer, Whitefield.

What a grand imposing church is All Saints, Stand. It reflects how prosperous the area was. There are many large monuments recording the illustrious families of the area in a packed churchyard.

All Saints Church, Stand. This card was obviously taken to show the unusual feature of the church. The tower base is external and open, giving ample shelter to church goers waiting for carriages after the service.

83

WITHINGTON

Two pictures of the same corner, on Wilmslow Road, Withington, showing the Scala Cinema. The first from about 1906, and the second is much later probably about 1948. The railings outside the cinema were probably taken for the War effort. The White Lion Hotel built in 1881 by William Mellor is featured on the later picture and is now known as the Withington Ale House.

The Village, Withington.

WITHINGTON

Wilmslow Road, Withington showing The Manchester and County Bank and Withington Methodist Church next to it. The Church was built in 1865 at a cost of £3,000 and could seat over 700 people. The bank wasn't doing too well as it let out part of it's frontage as two shops, maybe that idea could catch on again and bring bank charges down.

Wilsmlow Road, Withington East looking at the Village from Manchester. The block of buildings on the right are still standing. There is a large junction on the right now, just where the horse trough is in the picture. Withington Library is on that corner, not yet built when this picture was taken.

WORSLEY

Coffee Tavern, Worsley.

The building in the middle of this card was originally Worsley Delph Post Office in 1905 and the Packet House is behind the trees on the left. The entrance to the Duke of Bridgewater's under-ground canals is through the bridge, centre. The Coffee Tavern is behind the trees on the right, and is now a Restaurant.

Still surviving as a Civic Hall and Library Worsley Court House is situated by the roundabout at the entrance to the M62 slip road. Conveniently dated on the front as February 10th 1905 the building is not in fact much older.

WORSLEY

The Mill Brow Cafe in Worsley, about 1930. The party sat outside enjoying their tea perhaps arrived on that little bus or charabanc as they called them.

Worsley Village approached from Winton. The Bridgewater Hotel is just out of shot but you can see the signboard on the left. The cottages on the left were later adapted as shops. This is Barnton Road, Worsley in the mid-1930's.

WYTHENSHAWE

This picture of Wythenshawe Hall taken some time between the Wars. This is another fine hall that is being left to go to ruin for lack of cash. The Park surrounding the Hall is very popular with people from all over Manchester, there is a lovely walled garden and aviary. Both Hall and Gardens really deserve a bigger effort to be saved for the recreation of the people of Manchester.

WHIT WALKS

The Whit Walks were such an important part of Manchester tradition. Pictures of them show not only the different areas, but reflect the economic climate, and social history over the years. We have put the Whit Walk pictures from all over Manchester together under one section. Most of the pictures are self explanatory; Look closely at the proud smiling faces, you might even be in one yourself! I hope they bring back pleasant memories.

P.S. If you see yourself on any of these cards, please do tell us. Address on page 2

Three young ladies from St. Brides Church Old Trafford smile proudly at the camera in 1953. Note the ribbon again and the long gloves. People would beg steal or borrow to kit their children out for the Walks.

St. Mary's Methodist Sunday School, Moston walking in the Newton Heath Walks 21st May 1948.

WHIT WALKS

This picture showing the Hulme Walks in 1926. The walkers from St. Wilfreds Hulme, with the walkers from St. Agnes behind them. Look at the big lillies that the girls are carrying, and their long gloves which were traditional. Taken as they walked down St. Marys Street passing the corner of Halston Street, St. Marys Church can be seen in the background.

The neat, well-dressed procession ready to set out. The Whit Walks in Audenshaw, 1907. Love the hats

WHIT WALKS

Eccles Whit Walks 1935 and three young ladies representing St. Andrews Church have been singled out for this nostalgic shot. Note the hair-bands. One lovely point is the ribbons between the tinies which they were ordered to hang on to, to help them keep in some semblance of formation.

King Street is now buried under the Arndale Centre in Stretford, but here the Whit Walks of 1963 (probably starting from nearby St. Matthew's) are led by what looks like the Urmston Silver Band.

WHIT WALKS

WHIT WALKS
HULME
MANCHESTER
1920's

Although this is put as a Whit Walk, it really isn't. This picture compares with the previous pictures will show you that no matter how poor, children would have been better dressed than this at the Whit Walks. The black stockings really lay the seal on it, as no one would have worn these for Whit Walks. It is probably an outing from a school in the Hulme area in about 1920. It is a very interesting picture though.

THE LANGUAGE OF STAMPS

I came across a postcard around 1900 with "Please don't place the stamp upside down". I wondered about that and started to look for upside down stamps on the back of my postcards. I found one or two, but I also found some in other corners, and some stuck on at odd angles.

Then, in a book on the social history of Britain, I found the full explanation. Like S.W.A.L.K. (Sealed With a Loving Kiss) and I.T.A.L.Y. (I Trust and Love You) on the back of envelopes, it was a code. This 'stamp code' was normally used by courting couples in late Victorian and Edwardian times when the postcard craze was at its peak. Because postcards were so open and easily read by all, a 'hidden message' language grew up.

It was not 'the done thing' for a young lady to beg a young man to write to her, but if she put an upside down stamp in the opposite corner she could get her message across.

Lovers could always use their own version of this code to do their courting and wooing under their parents noses. You must remember that everyone sent postcards to everyone else. Cousins and friends wrote weekly, or even more often to each other. There were no phones, so postcards were the chatty way of keeping in touch. A postcard from a young man or a young lady was usual an acceptable but a letter was a serious business so the courting couple stuck to postards with the hidden message in the stamps.

I wonder if the next time I pay my electricity bill I stick the stamp sideways in the bottom left corner they may take the hint?

Top, Left-Hand Corner

I hate you

Good-bye for the present

My heart belongs to another and can never be yours

I love you

Top, Right-Hand Corner

My heart is given to another write to me no more

Do you love me, dearest

A kiss

Business

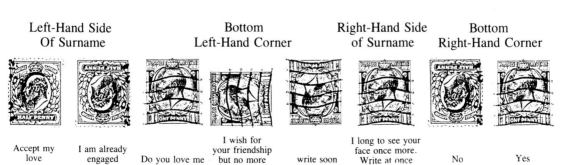

Left-Hand Side Of Surname

Accept my love

I am already engaged

Bottom Left-Hand Corner

Do you love me

I wish for your friendship but no more

Right-Hand Side of Surname

write soon

I long to see your face once more. Write at once

Bottom Right-Hand Corner

No

Yes

Manchester
Yesterday
&
Today

Stockport
Yesterday
&
Today

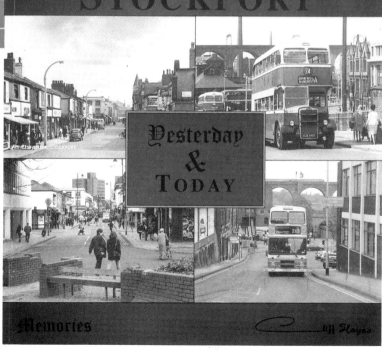

MANCHESTER TRAMS & BUSES

Ted Gray

Manchester
Trams
&
Buses

A Hundred Years of
The Manchester
Ship Canal

A Hundred Years of
THE MANCHESTER SHIP CANAL

Ted Gray

Also Available

£5.95

£5.95

A Memories publication